WHAT READERS ARE SAYING ABOUT
THE REFRAME GAME

"*The Reframe Game* is a fun and educational book filled with valuable tools for people of all ages. This book helps you to turn negative beliefs into positive ones. The information that has been so generously and lovingly offered can help to heal the soul deep within. It is absolutely a 'must own'!"

— **Cathy Webster**, educator

"*The Reframe Game* is easy to understand, insightful and infused with loving energy. It talks to anyone. I didn't want to put it down. It is joyful, helpful and uplifting. This is truly a guide to learning how to be more loving to yourself. Change yourself and you change the world."

— **Pat Kelley**, personal caregiver

"*The Reframe Game* explains a simple way to change your thinking. It is easy to understand and practice. As I use the Reframe Game I notice things shifting in my life for the better."

— **Arielle Sophia**, sales manager

"This book is a short, easy read that gives comfort and solace. **The Reframe Game** explains a simple teaching that each person can use to change his or her world. As a result our larger world will follow and change too. Everyone can reframe for peace, good health, and abundance. WOW!"

— **Barbara Stafford**, teacher, massage therapist & artist

"*The Reframe Game* is an easy guide for creating peace and happiness that is helpful for everyone –parents, teens and therapists. If you want to redirect your life in a more positive direction, this book is for you."

— **Laurie Sullivan**, reflexologist/therapist

"In **The Reframe Game,** the authors present a simple yet effective system to help you in your thinking. I highly recommend this book."

— **Kenny Baroff,** president, Marketing Plus One

"The Reframe Game is a book to help your life. This book can help anyone."

— **Matt Liss**, fishmonger

"Are you dreaming of a better life? The Reframe Game will teach you the basics of finding the positive words that you can use to be more loving to yourself. Your positive self-talk can indeed change your world in many wonderful ways."

— **Nina Ricci**, college alumni relations coordinator

"Whether you call it 'looking on the bright side' or 'the power of positive thinking,' Dr. Alexis Barron and Michelle Magid in The Reframe Game have captured the concept of reframing one's thoughts for easy use. The concise text and the clear, helpful reframes will help every reader access that loving peaceful spirit that resides in us all. When you are ready to change your world, read and use this book. It will become your handy tool towards peace and happiness."

— **Barbara Braun-McDonald**, psychiatric nurse, child therapist

"Dr. Alexis Barron and Michelle Magid don't just talk about affirmations; they offer a tool that will help you change your thoughts into kind and loving words."

— **Barbara Segal**, child and family therapist

"As we travel through this world most of us reach a point where we think, "there's got to be a better way!" We all want to be happier...less angry and frustrated...less worried about money, more content in our work, and blessed with good relationships. Yet we just don't know where to begin. When we decide to make changes in our lives, we need a plan, an accurate map, and the willingness to let go of our erroneous beliefs about ourselves. The Reframe Game provides us with everything we need to achieve our goal and remember who we 'really' are. This clear, concise and positive book reflects the simple Truth about us. We 'are' the extension of Love Itself and can learn to remember, practice and embrace our magnificent heritage."

— **Rev. Marcia M. Chapin**, D.Div., facilitator, A Course in Miracles

THE
REFRAME
GAME

THE
REFRAME
GAME

Create Peace and Happiness by Changing Your Thinking

Dr. Alexis P. Barron and Michelle Magid

A&M Press

THE REFRAME GAME

Create Peace and Happiness by Changing Your Thinking

A & M Press
P.O. Box 1155
Orleans, MA. 02653
800-528-4896

www.TheReframeGame.com

A Note to the Reader

Neither the publisher nor the authors are giving professional advice or services to the individual reader. The ideas, exercises and suggestions contained in this book are not intended as a substitute for medication, or for consulting with your physician, professional counselor or spiritual advisor. Neither the authors nor the publisher shall be liable or responsible for any loss, injury or damage allegedly arising from any information or suggestion in this book.

First Edition, 2010
Library of Congress Control Number 2010905854
ISBN 978-0-9826496-02
Printed in the United States

ATTENTION: EDUCATIONAL, THERAPEUTIC, AND SPIRITUAL INSTITUTIONS: Quantity discounts are available for the purchase of this book for educational purposes, reselling, gifts or subscription incentives. For information, please contact us at: www.TheReframeGame. com, or at our Sales Department at P.O. Box 1155, Orleans, MA 02653 USA, 800-528-4896.

May we all be at peace.
May we all be happy.

CONTENTS

Chapter 4

ACKNOWLEDGEMENTS

We would like to acknowledge our families, friends, colleagues, advisors and students for their inspiration, support and love while we have been writing our book. Thank you and we love you.

PREFACE

The seeds for this book were first planted when we met at a Buddhist retreat with Thich Nhat Hanh several years ago. We felt that we were supposed to work together to share with others the message that inner peace leads to world peace.

Our individual pain, suffering and inner turmoil had brought each of us to this spiritual retreat. Individually we had both suffered from the effects of childhood trauma. We have come to know and understand that true peace, self-love and happiness were not only possible, but also who we truly are. We have finally given ourselves permission to love ourselves.

Our purpose became to share our healing with others. Our healing helps others to heal. Peace and love are within all of us. We have seen how our peace brings peace to others, how our love brings love to others.

In our book we use the word God to refer to the love inside of us that connects us to universal love. Please use any word that works for you, e.g., the Divine, Source, Goodness, Love, Universe, Spirit, etc. We use the term "loving words" to describe language that is positive and makes us feel good about ourselves. We use the term "unloving words" to refer to language that is negative and makes us feel badly about ourselves.

Having studied human behavior much of our lives, we were always trying to understand human suffering, especially our own. After all our years of research, experience, reading, workshops and studying with spiritual teachers, these are the guiding principles that have helped us the most.

I am responsible for my life.

My thoughts and beliefs about the world and myself create my suffering or bring me peace and happiness.

If I change my unloving words to loving words about myself, others or life, then I can feel peace, love and happiness.

In order for my outer world to change, I must change my inner world.

Sometimes while writing this book our individual journeys have been uncomfortable. Many thoughts and beliefs arose that kept us from loving ourselves more fully, and these continue to come up for our consideration, examination and healing.

Noticing what we are saying to ourselves has become a practice for both of us. We have become keenly aware of how our self-talk makes us feel. Do we feel defeated, worthless, ashamed, resigned, anxious, depressed, sad, disempowered and victimized? Or do we feel worthy, proud, courageous, deserving, peaceful, energized, happy and self-confident?

We are learning the power in choosing our words wisely. This is a worthwhile process, even though it is not always comfortable. At times it has been difficult for both of us to become aware of some of our negative thinking habits. Ultimately, we are responsible for choosing our thoughts. By choosing loving thoughts and words we can better love ourselves and be at peace.

We are not the same Alexis and Michelle who first started writing this book. We have discovered that as we have been working on this book, this book has been working on us. Now we have even more inner peace, love and happiness. Our lives continue to improve steadily as we use more positive, loving language.

∞

INTRODUCTION

This book is the result of our intention to share with others how we have learned to create inner peace and happiness in our daily lives. Through our experiences we have come to realize that we are all wonderful. We are all good. Our essence is love and goodness. At our core there is nothing wrong with us. We are all okay. We are all born innocent and pure. Just look at a sleeping newborn baby. That peace and serenity is our birthright. It is who we truly are, our heritage.

Yet our negative, unloving language about our circumstances and ourselves can disconnect us from that love and goodness. It can hide our true spirits, our light. Our thoughts, our beliefs, and our stories can connect or distance us from the greatness that is in each and every one of us. It is our choice. By what we choose to tell ourselves we can feel frightened or comforted, abandoned or supported, unloved or loved, degraded or valued, anxious or calm, incompetent or self-confident, unhappy or content.

We discovered that when we became aware of what we were thinking and telling ourselves, we could change it. We are not powerless. We are not victims. We are not stuck with our negative thinking. As we changed our negative, unloving self-talk to positive, loving language, we began to have more inner peace and happiness. We became more present to our true selves, our inner goodness. In addition, the various areas of our life including family, work, and finances were not only improving but also bringing us more satisfaction.

So we started sharing this process of noticing what we are saying to ourselves with each other, as well as others. Consequently, the Reframe Game was developed. Reframing changes our negative, unloving thoughts to positive loving thoughts. To reframe means to look at something in a new way, from a different perspective. We use language turn-arounds and affirmations as reframes. The Reframe Game is a practical tool used to increase peace and happiness within ourselves. We have chosen to call it a game to make the process of changing our thinking more fun, simple and easy. In the following pages, we will introduce you to the Reframe Game, teach you how to play it, and provide reframe examples for the many areas of your life.

We invite you to entertain the idea that the Reframe Game will positively change your life, and that with the help of this book you can reframe your thinking to improve any area of your life. We have witnessed how the Reframe Game helps people to break through old entrapping thought patterns and habits. The Reframe Game is helping people live the life of their dreams, the life they were meant to live. It is our hope and belief that this book will help you simply and easily practice a more positive way of thinking, one that brings peace, happiness and other great rewards.

When we reframe we find it helpful to just relax, and to temporarily suspend any doubt and skepticism that may arise. We invite you to be patient and loving with yourself, as we have learned to do. Just take it one step at a time. Liberate the kid inside, that loving innocent child, and just have some fun with it!

We have opened this book with our own stories of how playing the Reframe Game has changed us. We have seen how the Reframe Game helps to increase energy, passion and prosperity as well as personal achievement, fulfillment, optimism, fun and personal esteem. We all deserve peace and happiness, and all the goodness that this game brings. We all deserve to feel good and have a wonderful life.

We believe that we are all beautiful souls who are innately good and have always been deserving of love, peace and happiness. We are born in the likeness of love and good, God and the Divine, and we are always connected to that place.

It is our negative unloving thoughts and beliefs about ourselves that keep us from feeling that connection. As we change those negative and unloving words about ourselves to loving ones, we can return to that place of love. We feel that connection to our innate goodness; it is our birthright to feel good.

The time is now, we invite you to say YES to loving yourself…

May you give yourself permission to be gentle, kind and loving to yourself, as we have.

Have fun!

Love to you,
Alexis and Michelle

ALEXIS AND THE REFRAME GAME

M y awareness of the power and influence of my self-talk began about 15 years ago with a significant wake-up call. I was complaining to a friend, "I am so tired, and I have so much to do." My friend did not commiserate with me, or even reinforce my "poor me" feelings. Instead she said to me, "Of course you're tired, because that is what you keep telling yourself." I was quite shocked. She was right. What I was telling myself actually made me more tired and miserable.

My friend, on the other hand, was telling herself how much she loved her life. She would literally chant several times a day, "I love my life. I love my life." She really did enjoy her life, and seemed to have an abundant supply of personal energy. I came to realize that I was talking to myself all the time. What I was saying to myself had the power to make me feel better or worse. Constantly saying I was tired did not make me feel any better; in fact my words were actually making me feel worse. My self-talk was negative and I was getting negative results. Yet I saw that my friend's language was positive and she was creating positive situations in her life.

It also seems that my body listens to every word I say. I used to get several miserable colds a year that would last for weeks. I would even worry about getting sick. One day when my youngest son was about 10 years old, he set me straight. I had looked at him and asked, "Are you getting a cold?" He seemed to be a little run-down. He gave me a very emphatic "No"! He then chanted: "I am healthy, I am healthy, I am healthy!" He didn't catch a cold. Through him I have learned the value of affirming that I am healthy.

Because I give more time and awareness to how I feel, I can now respond sooner. At the first sign of a cold I have learned to rest, eat well, and take things to enhance my immune system. But what seems to work best is my positive language. "I am healthy and cold-free."

I have also benefited in another health area of my life with the Reframe Game. For many years during the sunlight-deficient winters on Cape Cod where I live, I have experienced low energy – physically, mentally and emotionally. Besides exercise, supplements and additional light, what I say to myself becomes key.

When I notice that my energy is low, I say, "Cancel and erase" which is part of the Reframe Game. I then lovingly say to myself: "I am developing my inner sunshine." Since I have started using these wonderful words, the quality of my winters on Cape Cod has improved dramatically. I have more energy and lightness for all areas of my life.

Lastly, I love what the words "cancel and erase" do for me. When I can cancel and erase it allows me to start over, any time that I observe myself using negative, unloving words. When I say or think, "Cancel and erase," my fears can be replaced, nixed and banished. "Cancel and erase" changes my energy from negative to positive. I feel better. I can see my situation and myself with more love.

Several years ago, when I was starting my summer rental business, I would worry about a lot of things, including getting enough rentals, having good renters, and getting the property rental ready. Saying, "Cancel and erase" would allow me to easily and effectively deal with any fear that I had.

For example, I was afraid that potential renters would be unruly and damage the property. Using the Reframe Game I say, "Cancel and erase. I am attracting only angels as renters," allowing me to cancel my fearful, negative language. I am then free to choose more positive, loving words that make me feel better, and help me create wonderful things in my life. I have had wonderful renters – angels – for the last six years at our "Heavenly Family Retreat."

With the Reframe Game I am learning to use words that help me have more love for myself, so I can better love myself in all the areas of my life. Now I choose words that comfort, support and encourage me, instead of words that could scare, criticize or discourage me.

The Reframe Game has definitely helped me in my life. I have become more aware of what I am saying to myself. By choosing more positive, loving words, I now know that I can change what is happening in my daily life in simple easy, ways. I can do better, and feel better. In addition, the Reframe Game helps me to have more peace and happiness.

MICHELLE AND THE REFRAME GAME

While growing up, I developed false beliefs about myself and my world-at-large. These beliefs held me back from feeling peaceful and happy inside. The impetus for this book was for me to share the wisdom I am gaining as I learn to free myself from these old, worn-out, negative beliefs about my life and myself.

After surviving a life-threatening illness I looked deeply into my soul. I asked myself many questions: What has to change in order for me to feel good inside? What is keeping me hostage from feeling good about myself? Why am I not happy?

My inner dialogue was unloving and judgmental. Instead of loving and accepting myself, I was being hard on myself. I was the victim of my own negative thinking and wasn't even aware of it. I looked at the world through the eyes of a victim; fearful thinking that blamed my suffering on the outside world.

I continued to peel the layers of the onion to get to the heart of things. I had a deep realization that if I wanted to feel peaceful and happy inside, I would have to change my negative thinking. What I was thinking was creating how I was feeling.

I needed to take responsibility for feeling good. Nobody else could do that for me. Peace and happiness had to begin with me. For my outer world to look happier, I needed to change my inner landscape. Many of my stories were woven together from those old, worn-out past beliefs and perceptions.

Changing one belief at a time changed me from the inside out. As I changed my beliefs, my beliefs changed me. Understanding that I had choice in what words I could say to myself was incredibly empowering.

The Reframe Game became an effective way to change my negative beliefs to positive ones. At first, the Reframe Game wasn't always fun and easy, yet the more I played it, the more fun it became and the easier it was to change my thinking.

Reframing my unloving thoughts about myself with loving thoughts was quite a powerful tool. Instead of habitually saying, "I wish that I were different," I would cancel and erase and replace it with "I am fine just the way I am."

I noticed that the more I used these loving words, the stronger I felt inside. This strength helped me to move forward in my life. The more aware I was of what I was saying to myself, the more empowered I was to choose my words wisely.

One phrase I noticed myself saying again and again was, "I am overwhelmed." I would reframe that phrase to tell myself, "I take one step at a time." The more I said that, the less overwhelmed I felt. The Reframe Game became a valuable tool to use in my healing process to create peace and happiness inside of me. As I brought loving words to myself I felt more at ease. Little by little, I changed my old ways of thinking, and now it has become my practice.

For example, I had a fun opportunity to practice the Reframe Game at my bank. The bank teller told me that anyone who made a deposit that week would be eligible for a cash prize. Before using the Reframe Game I would have said, "I'll put my name in the drawing but I doubt that I will win." This time, being aware of my thinking, I said to myself, "I know that I am going to win this drawing." I proceeded to enter my name. As I handed my slip of paper with my name on it to the bank teller, I said with confidence and a great big smile, "I am going to be the winner of this drawing." I was affirming what I did want. A week later I received a phone call from the bank, telling me that I had just won the cash drawing.

By no means am I saying that every time I say something positive about what I want to happen, it actually happens. It is my experience that the more I practice the Reframe Game, the better I feel about myself, others and my life. Each time I reframe my negative self-talk to positive self-talk I am increasing that "good vibration" inside myself. I become a more positive magnet to attract that which I choose to have in my life. Positive thought brings positive changes.

Though today I am a changed woman, I see myself as a work in progress. By reframing my thinking, I am better able to look at life and myself through the eyes of love. I used to think that loving myself was selfish. I see things quite differently now. I now believe that it is the greatest gift I can give to myself.

The Reframe Game continually helps me to become aware of my thinking habits. It empowers me to live in the present moment. It is in that moment I am able to start fresh and new. It is in that moment I can reframe and choose my thoughts, using loving words that bring me peace and happiness.

Changing one belief at a time, one thought at a time – it really works!

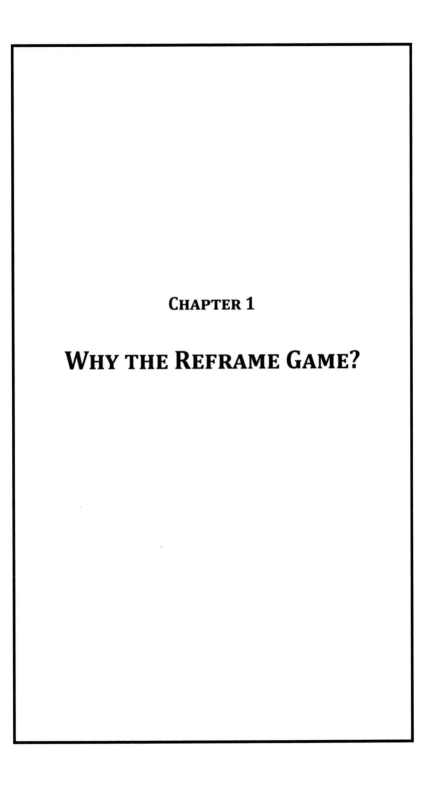

CHAPTER 1

WHY THE REFRAME GAME?

1
WHY THE REFRAME GAME?

D o you want to change your life? Do you want to feel better about yourself? The Reframe Game is an exciting way to make those changes happen. The Reframe Game is a cognitive tool for changing your thinking. Our thoughts guide our actions in the world. Since our thinking precedes our actions in the world, our positive thoughts help to inform our actions and thereby better ensure positive outcomes in our lives.

To reframe means to look at something in a new way, from a healthier and happier perspective. Poetically it is learning to look at ourselves, others and our lives through the eyes of love.

The Reframe Game uses the language of the heart, the language of love. With the Reframe Game you can choose to change your unloving, negative thoughts and words about yourself and your circumstances to loving, positive thoughts and words.

The power in your thoughts and words

We have thousands of thoughts a day. The Reframe Game is about becoming more aware of what we are thinking or saying to ourselves— our inner dialogue. What you are saying to yourself is very important. Your words have incredible energy and power. Your thoughts and words affect your mind, your body and your spirit.

Your words can activate particular areas of your brain that trigger your body to release certain chemicals that affect how you feel both positively and negatively.

Our thoughts help to determine our reality. If you want your life to improve, we encourage you to change your thinking. What you think about persists. If you keep thinking and complaining that something is or is not happening you could be actually creating or reinforcing that very condition.

Remember – your thoughts have energy. Similar energies attract like energies. For example, if you focus on how little money you have, then you will have little money. Instead, try saying, "I easily receive money in many ways." This positive statement will help attract more money. You are now focusing on abundance – rather than scarcity.

Thought precedes action. When we change our thoughts, our actions change. Our positive, loving thoughts and words will improve and enrich our lives.

We have found that what we say to ourselves can make us feel good inside or feel badly about ourselves. For example, try saying aloud or to yourself: "I am stupid." How do you feel? Do you feel competent or ignorant? Are you happy or sad? How do your insides feel? Is your body relaxed or tense? Do you want to be around other people? How is your energy? Do you feel ready to go or deflated?

Now try saying aloud or to yourself, "I am smart." Take a minute to check in with yourself. Say it again, "I am smart." How does saying, "I am smart" make you feel? Are you smiling? Are you relaxed? Are you standing taller? Do you feel competent and ready to deal with the next thing? Which statement works better for you, the positive or the negative?

Have you ever noticed that when you are around a person who is speaking negatively, you start to feel negative and out of sorts yourself? In comparison, hearing the positive words of another can uplift you. Well, it is the same with what you say to yourself.

You can weigh yourself down with your words or uplift yourself. Your words can scare you, or your words can comfort you. It is your choice. You are ultimately responsible for the words that you choose to use and believe.

The benefits of the Reframe Game

The Reframe Game can change your negative, unloving words about others, your circumstances and yourself. We have seen how the Reframe Game transforms our inner critic, that negative inner dialogue that interferes with our feeling of self-worth. As you become more aware of what you are saying to yourself, you will be able to choose what you want to say. This will allow you to be more kind and understanding to yourself and others.

When we use positive loving words, our relationships with ourselves, our family and our friends become easier and more rewarding. Our work is more enjoyable, creative and productive. There is less drama in our life. We have more peace and happiness. We feel calmer, joyful, happy, valued, proud and empowered.

The Reframe Game will help you to:

- Become more aware of your positive and negative thoughts
- Take responsibility for what you choose to say
- Let go of the past, and live in the present moment
- Reduce your stress, fear, anxiety, anger and depression
- Restore and renew your love for yourself, others and your circumstances
- Increase your inner peace, joy and happiness
- Create the life of your dreams

It's all about love

Several years ago we developed the Reframe Game to increase our self-love. We had become keenly aware that our mental suffering was the result of our negative self-talk. We were both tired of feeling badly because of what we were saying to ourselves. The Reframe Game allowed us to lighten up, and have some fun learning to love ourselves.

We are often very hard on ourselves. As we judge ourselves we keep love out. We may even start to believe that we are unlovable and unloved. We hope that you will find, as we did, that the Reframe Game helps to silence the inner critic. You are then more able to hear your inner voice of love, and you are more able to be gentle with yourself. In time, your limiting beliefs about yourself can change.

With the Reframe Game, you can love and comfort yourself with your words, as we have seen many people learn to do. Our wish is that we all feel peaceful, happier, and more loving toward ourselves.

The basis of the Reframe Game is that we are born in the likeness of the Divine, God, Source, Goodness, Love, Universe, Spirit, etc. It is our birthright. We are always connected to that source, whether we are aware of it or not.

Love is your source

It is our negative, unloving thoughts and beliefs about ourselves others, and the world that keep us from remembering that truth and living from that place of love. As we change those negative, unloving thoughts and beliefs to positive, loving thoughts and beliefs we feel more connected to our source, which is love.

This source of love is inside each of us. It is not something that is external to us. Michelle remembers when she was in a spiritual study group. A fellow student turned to her quite confidently and said, "Michelle, God is not outside of you. God is inside all of us." Michelle recalls being quite stunned. After all, this was a totally new belief for her. How could that be? Yet with much inquiry and deep reflection she came to believe it as the truth.

Here is an exercise that has helped us both to get in touch with our inner source of love:

- Sitting or lying down, make yourself as comfortable as possible and gently close your eyes
- Allow your body and mind to relax
- Place your hand over your heart and slowly breathe in and out
- As you breathe in, smile, and imagine someone or something that you really love, that brings you great joy
- Let yourself relax into this loving connection
- Feel the presence of love inside of you
- This love is the presence of God, the Divine
- Let every breath deepen this connection in you
- When you are ready, allow your breath to return to its natural rhythm
- Open your eyes, and slowly begin to move your hands and feet, fingers and toes

Practice this exercise regularly. Remember that God – Love – is always inside each of us, and that we are all one.

Choosing to love yourself through your language

We have come to understand how our thoughts and words can separate us from our divine nature, that place of love inside of us. Whenever we are not feeling that connection to love, it's very likely that our inner critic – the voice of self-judgment – is strong. We encourage you to look at how criticizing and judging yourself may be lowering your self-esteem. For example, the statement, "I am not good enough," may keep you from feeling your inherent goodness. Are your unloving words making you feel undeserving and less than others, and decreasing your self-confidence?

Whenever you choose loving self-talk you are giving yourself permission to love yourself. You are choosing to believe in yourself, telling yourself, "I am good enough."

Positive self-talk messages will support you in moving forward in your life. At your core you are fine. You are worthy of love. You deserve love. It is your birthright.

For many of us, our unloving words have covered up our love, light and goodness. We have been conditioned by what others have said to us while we were growing up and being socialized in our culture. For example, "You'll never amount to anything." "You should be ashamed of yourself." "What's wrong with you?" While it is not helpful or necessary to shame or blame others, it is from those words that we have internalized their negative beliefs about ourselves. We urge you to ask yourself, "Have I become my worst critic, rather than my best supporter?"

We have learned that we have many layers of false beliefs about ourselves. We encourage you to let positive language bring you back to the path of loving yourself. Please consider the wisdom of the ages that it is only in learning to love yourself that you can love another.

We use the term "unloving words" to refer to language that is negative and makes us feel badly about ourselves. Using unloving words can make you feel miserable, depressed, anxious, afraid, unmotivated and powerless.

Contrastingly, we use the term "loving words" to describe language that is positive and makes us feel good about our life and ourselves. Using loving words uplifts and comforts your spirit, increases your self-esteem, elevates your joy, and motivates and energizes you.

Please note that your loving words will become more powerful and believable the more you practice saying them to yourself or others. This will help you to feel more connected to your words. That's when the change happens. You are developing a new habit.

CHAPTER 2

KEY CONCEPTS FOR UNDERSTANDING THE REFRAME GAME

2

KEY CONCEPTS FOR UNDERSTANDING THE REFRAME GAME

Breathe

We have found that our breath is an important tool in helping us to know what we are saying to ourselves. Connecting to our breathing brings us into the present moment. We can now observe what we are thinking, what we are saying to ourselves. Being in touch with our breath helps us to develop awareness of that inner dialogue.

We encourage you to observe how your breathing affects your state of mind. Proper breathing calms your mind, body and spirit, bringing you into a more relaxed state.

Take a moment to inhale some air into your lungs. Allow your belly to gently expand. As you exhale, your belly relaxes.

Do this several times, noticing how you feel. Sometimes you may be holding your breath, and you aren't even aware of it. You may have noticed that the more anxious you feel, the less you are aware of your breath.

Being in touch with your breath helps you to develop awareness. With awareness, you have the power to choose what you say to yourself.

Please see the Glossary for a description of a breathing technique that we have found helpful.

Become aware of what you are saying to yourself

We have discovered that many people are unaware that they have an inner dialogue or that they are telling themselves negative statements. We have found that when you become aware of your self-talk it allows you the opportunity to choose what you want to say to yourself. If you want to make changes in your self-talk we invite you to become aware of what you are already saying to yourself.

By listening to your thinking and what you believe to be true, you can see how your words are making you feel. Try to notice what you are saying to yourself. For example, you may be aware that you are feeling anxious. You notice that you are thinking, "I am worried about my future." This awareness gives you the choice to reframe what you are saying to yourself. It is simple and easy to reframe the fearful thinking to, "I am happy and peaceful in the present moment."

Questions you can ask yourself to increase awareness

- What am I thinking right now?
- Am I at peace?
- How am I feeling?
- Am I happy?
- Are my words negative or positive, unloving or loving?
- What stories am I telling myself?
- What are my beliefs about others, my life and myself?

Cancel and erase

We are not sure where we first heard this phrase, but it grabbed us immediately. "Cancel and erase" has helped many people shift their thinking.

"Cancel and erase" is a direction you can give yourself in any moment. It helps to clear, eliminate and neutralize the negative effects of unloving words, which are based on your unloving thoughts and beliefs. It is analogous to deleting something on your computer. "Cancel and erase" can banish negativity, giving you the opportunity to come back to the present moment and start fresh with what you are saying to yourself.

We have found that loving words have a higher vibration. It is our hope that as you use loving words you will feel better inside. As a result, you can attract more peace, love and happiness.

Our experience has also shown us that unloving words have negative vibrations. Consequently, you do not feel good about yourself when you use them. For example, when you say to yourself, "I can't do this," you feel discouraged, defeated and depressed. The goal is to cancel and erase your unloving words.

Reframe

Reframe means to look at something in a new way, from a different perspective. We use language turnarounds and affirmations as reframes. A language turnaround literally revises what you are saying about your circumstances and or yourself. It turns it around and changes your perspective. For example, "I have no money," becomes "I receive money easily."

Positive affirmations are similar to turnarounds. Affirmations are positive statements about what you would like for yourself. An example of an affirmation is: "I am calm and relaxed."

Reframes are powerful, loving, high-vibration statements or declarations of what we want for ourselves in our lives. When we reframe our language, we change our negative, unloving words to positive, loving statements about our circumstances and ourselves. We like to say, "No shame, no blame, reframe." Reframing is a practice and a commitment you are making to enhance your well-being.

We have provided examples of reframes in Chapter 4. The reframes are categorized into the following areas:

Personal

Spiritual

Family

Child

Relationship

Job/Work

Finance

Home

Creativity

Health and Well-Being

Play the Reframe Game

DIRECTIONS

- Breathe
- Become aware of what I am saying to myself
- Cancel and erase any negative, unloving words
- Reframe with positive, loving words

I take a deep **breath**. I **become aware** of what I am thinking and saying to myself. Is it negative and unloving or positive and loving?

If I do not feel peaceful or happy I am most likely saying negative, unloving words to myself. I then say, **"Cancel and erase,"** either silently or aloud, to neutralize the negative effects of my unloving words. Finally I **reframe** my negative, unloving words with positive, loving words.

Some reframe examples

I have an important job interview. I notice that I am feeling anxious. I am afraid to go. I am aware that my stomach is tense. When I listen to myself I hear myself saying: "I can't go on this interview. I am so anxious." I take a deep breath, and say, "Cancel and erase." I then replace my negative, unloving thoughts with positive, loving ones. "I am confident and calm for my interview."

∞

In another work situation, we remember a friend complaining to us that she felt unappreciated at work. After listening compassionately, we suggested that she start affirming to herself, "I appreciate myself and the work I do," reminding her that any changes must begin inside, and then the outside world will reflect those.

About two weeks later we received a phone call from that same friend. She told us that out of the blue, her manager told her that she appreciated all her hard work. Months later she was offered the position of manager in her own store. She continues to affirm, "I appreciate myself and the work I do," to herself, and continues to hear positive feedback from those she works with. The Reframe Game is fun and it works!

∞

Here is another story, from a friend. She remembers many years ago, when her family unexpectedly had to move out of the house that they were renting. She was fear-ridden. She walked around saying, "I will never find a home," and, "I will never have the money for a new home, even if I find one."

A very optimistic cousin of hers kindly pointed out that as long as she kept saying those fearful words, that's what she would get – no home. Her cousin suggested that she start saying, "I have found the perfect home," and watch what happens. At first she was reluctant, and a bit cynical that this would make any difference. (Her fear-based thinking was stronger than her love-based thinking.)

She finally decided to take up the recommendation and began to say, "I have found the perfect home, and I have the money to buy it." It took awhile, yet eventually she found herself believing it was true. Lo and behold, one month later she found the perfect home, and a very generous seller who was willing to work with her! Not only that, her family lent her the money for a down payment.

As she shifted her negative unloving beliefs, her outer world positively shifted.

Resistance to change

If there is one thing that we can count on it is CHANGE. Whether we like it or not, things change. Yet many of us resist change, and resist changing. Old patterns feel comfortable. It is what we are used to doing. The "same old, same old" is a real comfort for many of us. The unknown may feel scary and unfamiliar. At times having more loving thoughts about ourselves can feel uncomfortable.

In right time

Often we cannot control when or how certain changes will occur in our life. We need to trust that things happen for our highest good, and the highest good of others. We have personally come to believe that love rules the universal time line.

Miracles unfold because of the power of love. You and I are part of, not in charge of, the wonderful process of life. Love has its own time schedule. Things will change when they do, in right time.

Fake it till you make it

We have found that sometimes you have to "fake it till you make it," or act as if the reframe is what you actually believe. This may be challenging, when loving reframes seem to fly in direct opposition to our reality.

We ask you to be patient with yourself and the process. Through your commitment and perseverance, your loving reframes will change your reality, affirming what you do want versus what you do not want.

The following is an example of faking it till you make it. A friend of ours was complaining about her cluttered workspace. We noticed that she was continually saying, "I am overwhelmed with the mess on my desk." It seemed that the more she said this, the worst she felt, and her desk was still messy. Consequently, we encouraged her to think about how good she would feel when her desk was cleared.

We also suggested that she say the following reframe until her desk was uncluttered: "I organize my paperwork and I feel calm." Within a short period she was able to clean her desk and she felt great. "Fake it till you make it" had worked for her.

CHAPTER 3

QUESTIONS AND ANSWERS

3
QUESTIONS AND ANSWERS

When should I play the Reframe Game?

A good time for the Reframe Game is when you are aware that your self-talk, your inner dialogue, is negative or unloving.

What if I can't hear my inner dialogue?

Sometimes it takes effort, time and practice to hear what you are telling yourself. Some people practice by setting aside part of their day to notice what they are saying to themselves. Others will write down their thoughts as they notice them. One of the best ways to become aware of your self-talk is by simply connecting with your breath. Our breath brings us into the present moment where we can observe what we are telling ourselves. To help in this process there is a breathing exercise in the Glossary.

While you are developing your awareness and practicing these skills, start by simply noticing when you are not feeling good inside. Notice when you feel angry, anxious, fearful, etc.

What if nobody else in my family wants to play the game?

It is important to remember that the only person that we can change is ourselves. As we do our inner work, those around us may begin to notice the effect and want to know what we are doing to feel better, others may not.

I've tried the game a couple of times and I didn't feel better.

Like anything, it takes practice to produce positive changes; this is not a quick fix. After all, many of the unloving words that we are saying to ourselves have become a strong habit. We need time to re-program our thinking. It is helpful to recognize all of the small strides you are making. Imagine where you would be if you had not noticed, canceled and erased some of the negative thinking that you have already caught, thanks to the Reframe Game.

It's also possible that some resistance is working against you. Part of you may like your old ways of thinking and feeling, and resist changing. Remember – you do deserve to feel better.

I am having trouble thinking of reframes.
Do you have any suggestions?

Look at your negative, unloving words. What are the opposites of these words? Experiment with bold, loving, statements for what you do want in your life. You can also use the extensive list of reframe examples we have provided in the next section of this book.

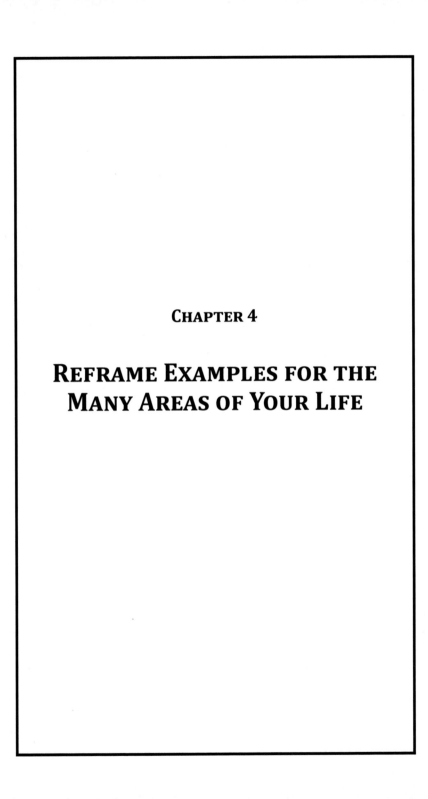

CHAPTER 4

REFRAME EXAMPLES FOR THE MANY AREAS OF YOUR LIFE

4
REFRAME EXAMPLES FOR THE MANY AREAS OF YOUR LIFE

In the following section of our book we have provided examples of reframes. Please feel free to make changes to these reframes or add your own. We have discovered that reframes require practice, commitment and action in order to work.

Remember that the first step in the Reframe Game is to breathe and become aware of what you are saying to yourself. When you notice that your words are negative and unloving, be sure to cancel and erase. Then replace your negative, unloving words with positive loving ones such as our examples. Have fun using the reframes to change your thinking.

Even if the statement in the reframe is not something that seems to be true for you now, act as if it is. This process will still work. Remember to "fake it till you make it!"

Reframes are provided for the following areas:

Personal

Spiritual

Family

Child

Relationship

Job/Work

Finance

Home

Creativity

Health and Well-Being

For your personal use, we have included blank charts called My Reframes at the end of the chapter. Have fun with them!

Personal Reframes

UNLOVING WORDS	CANCEL & ERASE	LOVING WORDS
I am afraid.	☼	I have courage.
I am angry.	☼	I calm myself. I choose to come from peace.
I feel isolated.	☼	I attract wonderful people to me.
I am anxious.	☼	Everything is just fine. I am calm.
I am ashamed of myself.	☼	I am proud of myself. I value myself.
I don't believe in myself.	☼	I accept myself. I believe in myself.
I blame others.	☼	I take responsibility for myself. I create the life that I want. I forgive.
I can't do anything right.	☼	I do my best in every moment.
I cannot do this.	☼	I can do this.
I don't like change.	☼	Change is part of life. I accept change.
Compared to others I am a failure.	☼	I am fine just the way I am. I am a work in progress.
I have no confidence in myself.	☼	I have confidence in myself. I am strong and capable.

Personal Reframes

UNLOVING WORDS	CANCEL & ERASE	LOVING WORDS
I am depressed/sad.		I reclaim my joy. I have vitality.
I wish that I were different.		I accept myself. I am fine just the way I am.
I have too much to do in such little time.		I have enough time. I prioritize.
I doubt myself.		I believe in myself. I have self-confidence.
I am not good enough.		I am good enough.
I am hard on myself.		I am kind and gentle to myself.
I am impatient.		I accept that things take time. I practice patience.
I am impulsive.		I think before I speak. I think before I act.
I am inadequate.		I am enough. I am competent.
I judge myself.		I accept myself. I have self-compassion.
I do not know what to do.		I ask for help.
I am overwhelmed.		I take one step at a time.

Personal Reframes

UNLOVING WORDS	CANCEL & ERASE	LOVING WORDS
I feel powerless.	☼	I reclaim my personal power. I have choices.
I settle for less.	☼	I deserve the best.
I am stupid.	☼	I am smart. I am brilliant.
I feel unappreciated.	☼	I appreciate myself. I value myself.
I am a victim of my circumstances.	☼	I take responsibility for my life and my choices.

Spiritual Reframes

In this book, the word God refers to the love inside of us that connects us to universal love. If the word God is not part of your belief system, please use any word that works for you, e.g., the Divine, Source, Goodness, Love, Universe, Spirit, etc.

UNLOVING WORDS	CANCEL & ERASE	LOVING WORDS
I feel abandoned by God.		God is always with me.
I feel all alone.		I am one with God.
I am angry.		I ask God for help.
I am anxious.		I trust in God. I am peaceful.
I need to be in control.		I relax. I let go and turn it over to God.
I feel guilty.		I forgive myself.
I do not know what to do.		I am open to God's help. I receive God's help.
I am powerless.		I find my strength in God.
I am scared.		I know that God is always with me.
I am worried about .... (name of person).		I put (name of person) in God's hands.
I am worried that this (name it) won't happen.		I trust in divine timing/God's timing.
I am not worthy of God's love.		God loves me unconditionally.

Family Reframes

In this section, the words child and parent are used as an example. However, child and parent can be replaced with mother, father, sister, brother, husband, wife, partner or any other family member.

UNLOVING WORDS	CANCEL & ERASE	LOVING WORDS
I worry about my child.	☼	I take appropriate action regarding my child.
I feel inadequate as a parent.	☼	I do my best as a parent.
I feel distant from my child.	☼	I make time to connect with my child.
I do not have a good relationship with my child.	☼	I express love to my child.
I see my child as a failure.	☼	I see the goodness in my child.
My child will not amount to anything.	☼	I look for the good in my child. I love and respect my child.
I judge my child.	☼	I take time to understand my child. I accept my child.
I do not know what to do.	☼	I ask for help.
I do not understand my child.	☼	I take time to listen to my child.
I have trouble communicating with my child.	☼	I communicate with love and kindness to my child.

Family Reframes
Reframes regarding personal self-care within the family

UNLOVING WORDS	CANCEL & ERASE	LOVING WORDS
I am so tired.	☀	I take time to rest.
I have no time for me.	☀	I choose to make time for myself.
I am overwhelmed.	☀	I take one step at a time.
My family life is stressful.	☀	I take good care of myself when I am with my family.
I have to please everyone.	☀	I am true to myself.

Child Reframes

UNLOVING WORDS	CANCEL & ERASE	LOVING WORDS
I don't like myself.	☀	I like myself just the way I am.
Nobody likes me.	☀	I like me!
Nobody loves me.	☀	I am loved.
I am no good at ____.	☀	I do my best.
I am stupid.	☀	I am smart.
I have trouble paying attention.	☀	I am learning to focus.
My mind wanders.	☀	I am learning to pay attention.
I am impulsive.	☀	I think before I act. I think before I speak.

Relationship Reframes

UNLOVING WORDS	CANCEL & ERASE	LOVING WORDS
I overreact in my relationships.		I take time to listen. I calm myself.
I act impulsively in my relationships.		I think before I act.
I am impatient with (name of person).		I take my time with (name of person).
If only he or she would change.		The only person I can change is me.
I judge (name of person).		I see and accept the goodness in (name of person). I take the time to understand (name of person).
I will never meet anyone who will love me.		I deserve to be loved.
My relationships are not working for me.		I choose to have healthy relationships.

New Job Reframes

UNLOVING WORDS	CANCEL & ERASE	LOVING WORDS
I will never get that job.	☼	I deserve to have a great job.
I am afraid to apply for that job.	☼	I have the courage to apply for that job.
I am afraid about this job interview.	☼	I have confidence that I will have a great interview.

Reframes for Working with Co-Workers

UNLOVING WORDS	CANCEL & ERASE	LOVING WORDS
I do not like working with (name of person).	☼	I find things to like about (name of person).
I judge (name of person).	☼	I take time to understand (name of person). I bring compassion to myself and others.

On-the-Job Reframes

UNLOVING WORDS	CANCEL & ERASE	LOVING WORDS
I am bored at my job.	☼	I find interesting things to do at my job.
I do not feel appreciated at work.	☼	I appreciate myself, and the work that I do.
I hate my job.	☼	I focus on what my job provides me. I can choose to find another job.
I will never get my work done.	☼	When I put my mind to it, I get my work done.
I am afraid of making mistakes.	☼	I do my best. I am compassionate with myself in all situations.
I feel pressured.	☼	I take things one step at a time.
I am overwhelmed by my paperwork.	☼	I organize my paperwork and feel calm.
I dread my job evaluation.	☼	I welcome feedback.
I procrastinate.	☼	I choose to just do it. I enjoy completing a job.
I work long hours, and I never see my family.	☼	I balance my time between family and work.
I am afraid that I will be laid off or downsized.	☼	There is a good job for me. I take appropriate action.

Finance Reframes

UNLOVING WORDS	CANCEL & ERASE	LOVING WORDS
I have no money.	☼	**I am deserving of money.** **I easily receive money in many different ways.** **I take appropriate action.**
I don't know how I am going to pay my bills.	☼	**I trust in the abundance of the universe.** **I take appropriate steps to pay my bills.**
I worry about not having enough money.	☼	**I am open to the flow of financial abundance.** **I attract and receive money.**
I cannot afford that.	☼	**I am grateful for what I have.** **I choose to spend my money wisely.**
I wish that I had more money.	☼	**I create opportunities to increase my income.** **I focus on the abundance in my life.**

Home Reframes

UNLOVING WORDS	CANCEL & ERASE	LOVING WORDS
My home is full of clutter.	☼	I have a clutter-free home.
I am overwhelmed by my clutter.	☼	I deal with one item at a time.
My house is a mess.	☼	I make time to put things away. My home nourishes and supports me.
I am wasteful.	☼	I live simply and recycle. I use the earth's resources consciously.
There is too much work to do around my home.	☼	I focus on one thing at a time.
I cannot find a home to buy.	☼	I have found the perfect home.

Creativity Reframes

UNLOVING WORDS	CANCEL & ERASE	LOVING WORDS
I am not creative.	☼	I am open to my creativity. I am creative.
I can't .... paint, write, etc.	☼	I allow my creativity to flow.
I am blocked in my painting, writing, etc.	☼	I have fun exploring my creative side.
I don't deserve to take time to be creative.	☼	I value my creative self.
I have no time to be creative.	☼	I make time for my creative work.
I am afraid to show my work.	☼	I show my work with confidence.
I procrastinate when it comes to being creative.	☼	I take one step at a time. I let go of perfection.

Health and Well-Being Reframes

Mind (mental health and well-being)

UNLOVING WORDS	CANCEL & ERASE	LOVING WORDS
I am stressed.	☼	I calm myself. I am relaxed.
I am anxious.	☼	I am at ease. I am at peace.
I am depressed/sad.	☼	I reclaim my joy. I have vitality.
I am worried about my future.	☼	I am peaceful and happy in the present moment.
I worry.	☼	I let go of worry. I am at peace.
I procrastinate.	☼	I enjoy completing things.

Health and Well-Being Reframes

Body (physical health and well-being)

UNLOVING WORDS	CANCEL & ERASE	LOVING WORDS
I am tired.	☀	I take time to rest.
I have no energy.	☀	I am filled with vital energy.
I have tension in my body.	☀	I relax my body.
I don't feel well.	☀	I take time to rest. I am strong and healthy.
I have unhealthy eating habits.	☀	I eat very well. I value eating healthy foods.
I do not like to exercise.	☀	I make regular exercise a priority.

My Reframes

UNLOVING WORDS	CANCEL & ERASE	LOVING WORDS
	☼	
	☼	
	☼	
	☼	
	☼	
	☼	
	☼	
	☼	
	☼	
	☼	

My Reframes

UNLOVING WORDS	CANCEL & ERASE	LOVING WORDS
	☼	
	☼	
	☼	
	☼	
	☼	
	☼	
	☼	
	☼	
	☼	
	☼	
	☼	

My Reframes

UNLOVING WORDS	CANCEL & ERASE	LOVING WORDS
	☼	
	☼	
	☼	
	☼	
	☼	
	☼	
	☼	
	☼	
	☼	
	☼	

My Reframes

UNLOVING WORDS	CANCEL & ERASE	LOVING WORDS
	☼	
	☼	
	☼	
	☼	
	☼	
	☼	
	☼	
	☼	
	☼	
	☼	

My Reframes

UNLOVING WORDS	CANCEL & ERASE	LOVING WORDS
	☼	
	☼	
	☼	
	☼	
	☼	
	☼	
	☼	
	☼	
	☼	
	☼	

My Reframes

UNLOVING WORDS	CANCEL & ERASE	LOVING WORDS
	⚡	
	⚡	
	⚡	
	⚡	
	⚡	
	⚡	
	⚡	
	⚡	
	⚡	
	⚡	

GLOSSARY

GLOSSARY

Here are some helpful explanations of the concepts behind the Reframe Game:

Affirmations

Affirmations are positive statements about what we would like for ourselves. We say these statements as if they are already true.

Becoming aware

We notice what we are telling ourselves. When we pay attention to our language, we can choose which words to use. We become aware of our self-talk, our inner dialogue.

> **Questions to help us become aware of what we are saying to ourselves:**
>
> How is my state of mind?
>
> What am I thinking at this moment?
>
> How am I feeling in this moment?
>
> Are my words loving or unloving?

Beliefs

Thoughts we think over and over become our beliefs, something we think is true. Our beliefs shape our perception of our world, others and ourselves. Changing negative beliefs about ourselves can change our lives in the most positive ways.

Blame

To blame is to hold someone else responsible for a fault, error or mistake. When playing the Reframe Game we take responsibility for our choices and ourselves in a loving way. Therefore we say, "No shame, no blame, reframe!"

Breathing

Breathing is inhaling air into our lungs and exhaling air out from our lungs. As we focus on our in breath and out breath we are brought into the present moment. As we practice becoming aware of our breath we will have more peace and happiness.

Breathing technique

The following breathing technique can help you to maximize the benefits of proper breathing. Initially, it helps to practice this while lying down with your hands on your belly. Breathing in, allow your lungs to gently fill with air, expand your diaphragm, and allow your belly to gently rise. As you exhale your breath, feel your belly and then your diaphragm gently relax and fall. Enjoy practicing breathing in and out for several minutes.

Cancel and erase

Cancel and erase is a phrase used to eliminate and neutralize the effects of our unloving language. Energetically, cancel and erase clears negativity. Cancel and erase redirects the mind, giving it something else to do.

Choice

Choice is the freedom to decide what we are thinking or what we want to do. Being aware of our thoughts allows us the choice to change them. Choosing loving thoughts instead of unloving thoughts brings us more peace and happiness. Choice gives us hope. We can always choose again, no matter where we are.

Compassion

Compassion is deep kindness and understanding for oneself or another. When we feel compassion, we speak lovingly without harsh criticism or judgment.

Deserving

We are already worthy. It is our birthright to have good things in all parts of our lives. We no longer have to punish ourselves or suffer. We deserve to feel good.

Fake it till you make it

Act as if something already exists. Act as if you know how to say or do something. Act as if you feel the way you would like to feel.

Fear

Fear can be expressed as anxiety, depression or anger. A commonly heard acronym for fear is that it is False Evidence Appearing Real.

Feng Shui of the mind

Clear and eliminate the clutter of the mind. This clutter consists of our negative, unloving and critical self-talk about our circumstances and ourselves. We invite peace, harmony and happiness into our lives when we eliminate negative thoughts.

Forgiveness

Forgiveness is to excuse or pardon. We are willing to let go of something that felt hurtful to us. We forgive so that we can be free.

God

We use the word God to define the love that is within all of us. Other names for this love can include the Divine, Source, Goodness, Universe or Spirit. We do not have to look outside of ourselves for God. God is inside each of us. God is love. When we are in touch with the love in our hearts, we touch the Divine. We are all one with this connection.

Happiness

Happiness can be defined as inner joy and contentment.

Inner light

Our natural state of love, goodness, peace and happiness that is always present.

Loving and accepting ourselves

Loving and accepting ourselves is tapping into the perfection of who we truly are – love. When we love and accept ourselves we value ourselves. We can be kind, gentle, comforting and supportive of ourselves. When we are hard on ourselves there is no room to feel this love; our unloving words block this love for others and ourselves. When we are unloving we are at war with ourselves. When we are loving we are at peace with ourselves. When we focus on the good inside of us we are more kind, understanding, gentle and compassionate.

Loving words

The term loving words refers to language that is positive and makes you feel good about your life and yourself. Using loving words uplifts and comforts your spirit, increases your self-esteem, elevates your joy, and motivates and energizes you.

Mental diet

A healthy mental diet means we let go of unloving words and choose loving words for peace and happiness. It allows us to feel much lighter.

Mental makeover

A mental makeover redesigns our negative, unloving mindset into a positive, loving mindset. Our positive, loving words restore and renew us.

Mental muscle

By playing the Reframe Game we strengthen our positive self-talk – our mental muscle. It's analogous to working out at a gym to build our physical muscles. By playing the Reframe Game we are strengthening our positive, loving mental muscle.

Mind check

Without judgment we tune in and ask ourselves, "Are my thoughts negative or positive, unloving or loving?"

Mind shifting

To change from using unloving words to using loving words.

Peace

Peace can be defined as inner calmness, tranquility, equanimity, and an absence of war. Peace can only begin with oneself. The outer world reflects our inner world of thoughts and perceptions. We can change the world by changing ourselves.

If you want peace, become peace. Inner peace brings world peace.

Perception

Perception is an insight or awareness. Perceptions are based on our thoughts and beliefs. Our reality is created by our perceptions. By using the Reframe Game we have an opportunity to change our reality by changing our perceptions.

Practice

To practice (verb) means to work repeatedly at something in order to become proficient. We practice the Reframe Game so it can become a habit. A *practice* (noun) is something that has become a recurring habit or activity. We develop a practice of choosing loving words.

Power in our words

Power means to have force or energy. Our words have power. *Loving words* are gentle, accepting, respectful, praising, cooperative, optimistic, reassuring, comforting, encouraging, calming, forgiving, unlimited, generous, joyful and peaceful. *Unloving words* are critical, judgmental, shaming, blaming, competitive, pessimistic, fearful, harsh, discouraging, anxious, unforgiving, limiting, lacking, resentful and condescending.

Please note that your loving words will become more powerful and believable the more you practice saying them to yourself or others. This will help you to feel more connected to your words. That's when the change happens. You are developing a new habit.

Reframe

Reframe means to look at something in a new way from a different perspective. Reframes are powerful, loving, high-vibration statements or declarations of what we want in ourselves or in our lives. In the Reframe Game we use language turnarounds and positive affirmations as reframes.

Self-compassion

Having self-compassion is a freedom from judging oneself, and it means treating oneself with loving kindness and understanding.

Self-judgment

Self-judgment is being critical of and hard on ourselves. Judging ourselves keeps us from knowing who we truly are – love and goodness. As we release our judgmental thinking and beliefs about ourselves, we are better able to hear the voice of love within us. Instead of asking what is wrong with us, we see what is right.

Self-love

Self-love is about appreciating and honoring the wonderful being that you are.

Self-talk

Self-talk is our internal dialogue – what we are telling ourselves.

Shame

Shame is a lack of pride and self-respect. Shame can hide our inner goodness.

Stories

We tell ourselves stories as narratives and commentaries about our daily lives. For example, we make ourselves the victim or the hero in our life. We tell our story as a drama, a comedy or a peaceful tale. As we reframe our everyday language with love, our lives can become the love stories that we deserve.

Unloving words

Language that is negative and makes you feel badly about yourself. Using unloving words can make you feel miserable, depressed, anxious, afraid, unmotivated and powerless.

CONCLUSION

We've come to the end of our book, but not the end of our story. We will continue, as we hope you will, to play the Reframe Game. We will continue to cultivate the practice of replacing our negative, unloving thoughts with positive, loving thoughts. And we will continue to remember that who we truly are is love.

Thank you for being with us on this journey.

Please visit our website: **www.TheReframeGame.com**

Love to you,
Alexis and Michelle

ABOUT THE AUTHORS

Alexis P. Barron, D.Sc., has spent more than 30 years as an educator. Her studies with many healers, spiritual teachers, and Feng Shui masters have complemented her doctoral degree in behavioral sciences from the Harvard School of Public Health, and her Masters degree in education from Lesley University.

She is committed to health and well-being, helping people of all ages discover and create peace, joy and happiness within themselves and in their environments. To achieve this end, she utilizes her diverse gifts as a health educator, behavioral scientist, Feng Shui consultant and spiritual teacher. She teaches and consults with individuals, groups, organizations, and corporations by providing classes, workshops, and lectures.

Born in New Jersey, Alexis now lives in Orleans, Massachusetts at the Heavenly Family Retreat, a vacation property she has created with her children on beautiful Cape Cod. Her greatest joys continue to be her three grown children, Matt, Anna and Alex, her spiritual practice, spending time in nature – especially in her garden, singing and dancing, and traveling whenever she can.

Website: **www.TheReframeGame.com**

Michelle Magid has her Master's Degree in Counseling Psychology from Lesley University in Cambridge, Massachusetts, as well as a combined undergraduate degree in Education and Child Psychology from Boston University. She has been working in the field of psychology for over 20 years. She is a Reiki Master and has a private practice integrating psychology, coaching, Reiki and intuitive guidance.

She has learned from her practice that when a person is re-directed from fearful thinking to love-based thinking, healing is possible on all levels. Children, teens, adults and animals can all benefit from this shift. She has found that the presence of love is the "all encompassing healer."

As an artist, she has studied at the Museum of Fine Arts, The Massachusetts College of Art in Boston, and the Provincetown Art Association and Museum. She was born in New Jersey and she currently lives on Cape Cod with her family, where she enjoys gardening, photography, music and the beautiful beaches.

Website: **www.TheReframeGame.com**

EASY ORDER FORM

Web orders: www.TheReframeGame.com

Telephone orders: call 800-528-4896
Have your credit card ready.

Postal Orders: A & M Press, PO Box 1155, Orleans, MA 02653 USA

Name: _____

Address: _____

City: _____ State: _____ Zip: _____

Phone: _____

Email: _____

Please send me _____ copies of *The Reframe Game.*

Payment: ☐ Check
          ☐ Visa   ☐ MasterCard   ☐ AMEX   ☐ Discover

Card number: _____

Name on card: _____

Exp. date: (mm/yy) _____

CPSIA information can be obtained at www.ICGtesting.com
Printed in the USA
LVOW06s1706020314

375734LV00027B/1617/P